Dedicated to my Daughter Aliya, Son Kristopher and Son Matthew. I love all of you very much! I wanted nothing more than to be a mom and am blessed to have been given three great kids! One born from me and two given to me, all of you very special and the reason I believe God put me on earth. He already knew when I was born who I would mother, what a wonderful God he is!

For all those children in foster care who live with or are adopted by families that are different races. We are all alike inside and that is where it counts!

Printed in the United States of America

ISBN-13: 978-1442132580

ISBN-10: 1442132582

Why Do I Look Different Mommy

by Karin Schermerhorn

Illustrated by Fátima Stamato

Tell me again Mommy.........
why do I look different than you?

Mommy why are my eyes brown, and your eyes are green and brother's eyes are blue

That's how God made us sweetie, you, your brother and me. He choose the color of your eyes and ours too. Just as he choose the color of your friends eyes and everyone else you see.

Tell me again Mommy.......
why do I look different than you?

My hair is black and hurts to comb, your hair is brown and soft and fun to do.

God made your hair just the way it is supposed to be my love, and he made mine for me.
We may be different but we are the same, you see?

**Tell me again Mommy......
why do i look different than you?**

My skin is brown and baby brother's too, but your skin is white just like big brother's too......

My daughter God made each of us the color outside that he wanted us to be. We may not look alike but our love is the same, God picked us out for each other and made us family.

Tell me again Mommy, why I look different than you? The other's in our family don't look like me, they look like you too?

That's true my love, you grew in your brown mommy's tummy and look like her, and her family does too.

You grew in my heart and now you see, we may not lok alike, but you are ours, your brother's and me!

Tell me again Mommy, I want to hear......
how I came to you and my brother
and how you love me so dear?

Oh this is a great memory to share,
how you came to us that day!
you came as a foster baby,
so tiny and new,
we knew right away
you would be all ours very soon!

Please tell me again Mommy,
I really want to know
what happened to my brown mommy
who kept me inside and let me grow?

Your brown mommy sweetie loved you
so,
she really wanted to stay with you and
help you grow.
But she was sick and it hurt her a lot,
she had to let you go and now you see,
you will always be OUR family!

**Tell me again Mommy what you say
when you tuck me into bed
at the end of the day....**

Just like your nana did with me,
and momma did
with your brother too.......

Now run along home and jump into bed.....

say your prayer's.....

and cover your head.....

the very same thing.....

I say to you.....

you dream of me.....

and I'll dream of you!!!!

Night night baby girl, I love you!

Made in the USA
Monee, IL
02 March 2021